The SIMPSONS LIBRARY of WISDOM

THE LISA BOOK

THE SIMPSONS™ LIBRARY OF WISDOM
THE LISA BOOK

Copyright © 2006 by
Matt Groening Productions, Inc. All rights reserved.

Printed in the United States of America.
No part of this book may be used or reproduced in any manner whatsoever without written permission
except in the case of brief quotations embodied in critical articles and reviews. For information address
HarperCollins Publishers,
10 East 53rd Street, New York, NY 10022.

HarperCollins books may be purchased for educational, business, or sales promotional use. For information please write:
Special Markets Department,
HarperCollins Publishers,
10 East 53rd Street, New York, NY 10022.

FIRST EDITION

ISBN-10: 0-06-074823-0
ISBN-13: 978-0-06-074823-4

07 08 09 10 11 WOR 10 9 8 7 6 5 4 3 2

Publisher: Matt Groening
Creative Director: Bill Morrison
Managing Editor: Terry Delegeane
Director of Operations: Robert Zaugh
Art Director: Nathan Kane
Special Projects Art Director: Serban Cristescu
Production Manager: Christopher Ungar
Production/Design: Karen Bates, Art Villanueva
Staff Artists: Chia-Hsien Jason Ho, Mike Rote
Production Assistant: Nathan Hamill
Administration: Sherri Smith
Legal Guardian: Susan A. Grode

THE SIMPSONS™ LIBRARY OF WISDOM

Conceived and Edited by Bill Morrison
Book Design and Production by Serban Cristescu
Contributing Editor: Terry Delegeane

Contributing Artists:
KAREN BATES, JOHN COSTANZA, ISABELLE CRISTESCU, SERBAN CRISTESCU, MIKE DECARLO,
FRANCIS DINGLASAN, LUIS ESCOBAR, NATHAN HAMILL, CHIA-HSIEN JASON HO, NATHAN KANE,
ISTVAN MAJOROS, JEANETTE MORENO, BILL MORRISON, KEVIN M. NEWMAN, JOEY NILGES,
ANDREW PEPOY, MIKE ROTE, KEVIN SEGNA, CHRIS UNGAR

Contributing Writers:
JAMIE ANGELL, TERRY DELEGEANE, JESSE LEON McCANN, BILL MORRISON, GAIL SIMONE, MARY TRAINOR

Special Thanks to:
Pete Benson, N. Vyolet Diaz, Deanna MacLellan, Helio Salvatierra, Mili Smythe, and Ursula Wendel

The SIMPSONS LIBRARY of WISDOM

THE LISA BOOK

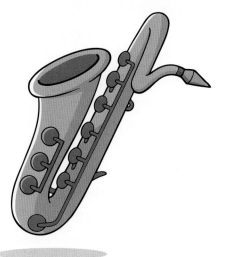

HARPER

NEW YORK • LONDON • TORONTO • SYDNEY

1. Spelling bees.
2. Pop quizzes.
3. Mensa practice drills.
4. Homework on weekends.
5. Great expectations.
6. Civil disobedience.
7. A worthy adversary.
8. Extended sax solos.
9. Public television.
10. Personal enlightenment.
11. Political correctness.
12. Overachieving.
13. Ponies (or even just one pony).
14. Angst.
15. Mom's pancakes.
16. Dad's jokes.
17. Maggie's smile.
18. Bart's absence.
19. This sweet Land of Liberty.
20. Sinatra gnawing man (winning at anagrams).
21. Yendor, Bubbles, Doofy, and Moldy.
22. Tofu hot dogs.
23. Bright copper kettles.
24. Warm woolen mittens.
25. Ice hockey.
26. Bleeding Gums Murphy.
27. Lawrence Ferlinghetti.
28. Herschel Krustofski.
29. Rebels with a cause.
30. Fries with a milkshake.
31. Releasing my inner howl through music.
32. TV commercials with raccoons in them.
33. Rising to the occasion.
34. Carpe-ing the diem.
35. The medulla oblongata.
36. Substitute teachers that care—really care.
37. Things that go "plink, plunk" in the night.
38. Underdogs.
39. Silver linings.
40. Smoking guns (figuratively).

LISA'S LIFELINE

FRETFUL MOTHER MAGAZINE
Is Your Baby Too Cute?

AGE: MONTHS BEFORE BIRTH
As fetus, strong cautionary sense instilled by pregnant Marge's worrisome reading matter: **Fretful Mother Magazine.**

AGE: THE FIRST DAY
A beautiful mind is born. Lisa's political leanings seem natural, considering day's newspaper headline: "Mondale to Hart: 'Where's the Beef?'"

AGE: THE FIRST WEEK
Becomes environmentally conscious, thanks to aunts' cigarette smoking/overly-abundant facial hair.

A hamlet is a village without a church. A town is not a city until it has a cathedral.

AGE: 6 MONTHS
Exciting "first" events: first visit with neighbors after Bart pushes her through Flanders' doggie door; first vacation, after Bart shoves her in mailbox, attempting overseas shipping; first hair styling, shaved bald by Mr. Bart of Evergreen Terrace.

AGE: 2 YEARS
Begins to realize no one notices/appreciates her talent/intelligence, despite ability to spell at eighth-grade level with wooden blocks. Luckily, Bart recognizes talent/enlists her to help pilfer cookie jar.

AGE: 1 YEAR
Parents' hands full with big brother, so Lisa learns early to walk/talk/change own diapers. First word is "Bart," followed soon by "Mommy"/"Homer"/"David Hasselhoff."

MAIL

MENSA

AGE: 3 YEARS
Parents/school administrators finally become aware of her special gifts; clues were ability to complete advanced math problems/puzzle of Taj Mahal. She's rewarded with first saxophone. Frustration with surrounding dimwitted populace somewhat abated.

AGE: 4 YEARS
First tragedy of young life as pet hamster dies in freak garbage disposal accident. Bart able to cheer her up by tricking Homer into biting his own finger repeatedly, thinking it's a hot dog.

AGE: 6 YEARS
Lisa has three articles published in **The New Yorker** under pseudonym Ms. Lizzie Strongheart; no one minds they are about dolphins/unicorns/jazz saxophone riffs, respectively.

AGE: 6 YEARS, 3 MONTHS
Two boys named Corey catch her eye on daytime soap opera; Lisa is smitten. Somewhere in neighborhood, Milhouse cries silently to himself, doesn't know why.

AGE: 5 YEARS, 4 MONTHS
Uses logical argument/convinces kindergarten teacher to quit job/join military. Everyone involved much happier.

AGE: 7 YEARS
In a moment of fleeting, unrepeatable scientific clarity, Lisa writes formula for cold-fusion generator in notebook; Santa's Little Helper eats notes when Bart uses her science kit to make "stink juice."

AGE: 5 YEARS
Begins school. Immediately discovers she's being stalked by weird older kid with big nose/glasses/blue hair. When she confronts mysterious stranger, he emits abnormal high-pitched noises then runs into Boys' Room.

AGE: 8 YEARS
Busy year: joins Mensa; learns to play hockey; brings down crooked politician; attends all-boy military school; travels to Calgary to compete in Spellympics; performs at jazz club; fakes way into college; becomes vegetarian/Buddhist. Despite all outward appearances, she's grown a lot.

AGE: 4 YEARS, 6 MONTHS
Discovers first-aid around same time big brother discovers skateboarding.

Leonardo da Vinci invented scissors (but he never ran with them).

The term "ökologie" (ecology) was coined in 1866 by the German biologist Ernst Haeckel. The word comes from the Greek "oikos," (household), meaning the study of the household of Nature.

1. Eat my Carob and Wheatgrass Shortbread Snacksters
     (rather than my shorts)!
2. X-tra credit...to the X-treme!
3. Oh, that's so Lisa! (Note: bribe popular kids to say this one.)
4. Hey, you got agar in my peanut butter!
5. Don't have a cow, man—try a delicious and cruelty-free
     tofu burger instead!
6. Sit on it, Potsie! (Note: taken.)
7. It's not just good, it's HALL PASS good!
8. You ARE the weakest link (but I'm available for tutoring on a
     sliding pay scale)!
9. I've got sax appeal!
10. I'll do your homework if you'll be my friend!
11. It's nonviolent conflict mediatin' time!
12. No tuna for ME, thanks!
13. Why, that's Jazztastic!
14. He's not MY dad!
15. I'm KOO-KOO for renewable energy resources!
16. Well, shut my mouth and call me a suffragette!
17. You can always bet on the Teacher's Pet! (Note: saying this on
     the playground carries the risk of an atomic wedgie.)
18. I'm smarter than the average "straight A" student!
19. Heavens to Trigonometry!
20. Sufferin' Lab Animals!
21. What's up, Jock?
22. Up, Up, and Read Poetry!

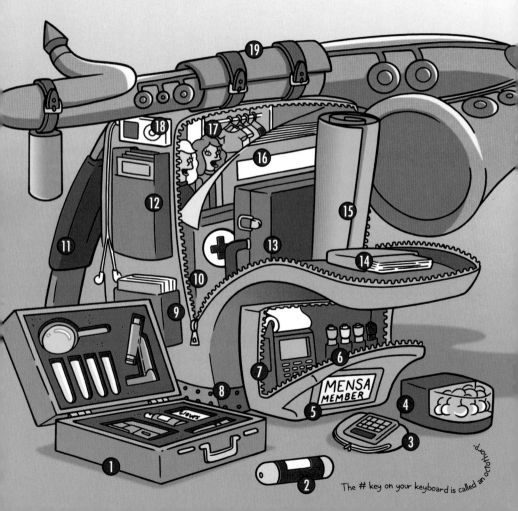

LISA'S ULTIMATE BACKPACK

The # key on your keyboard is called an octothorp.

1. Mobile science lab (in case an unsolved murder crops up on the playground; equipped with Luminol® spritzer).
2. Combination laser pointer/lip balm.
3. Coin purse/international currency converter (a must for trips to Ethnic Town).
4. Built-in automatic sonic pearl necklace cleaning device (runs off USB computer ports; side compartment holds back-up strand).
5. MENSA membership cardholder (for bragging rights).
6. Bank of color hi-liters (necessary for color-coding things).
7. Mega-calculator (computes π up to four hundred places; has universal language translator for all languages—even the dead ones).
8. Triple-reinforced Kevlar® bottom (prevents underside breakage due to excessive book weight; also bulletproof).
9. "Field Identification Guide to Cute, Fuzzy Animals and Their Habitats."
10. Li'l Florence Nightingale First Aid Kit™.
11. Ergonomic nonchafing straps.
12. Eject-O-Brochure Dispenser™ (handy when feminist and/or environmental pamphlets are needed at a moment's notice).
13. Bart-proof homework strongbox.
14. Pocket Oxford Dictionary (for when some pseudo-know-it-all absolutely, positively needs to be proven wrong).
15. Meditation mat.
16. Magazine pocket (contains recent issues of "Nonthreatening Boys," "Buddhism Today," and "Bluesweek").
17. Traveling Malibu Stacy closet (holds two dolls and hundreds of accessories; hidden compartment conceals dolls from older girls and stupid brother).
18. Built-in MP3 player with headphones (contains downloads of Coltrane, Monk, Bleeding Gums Murphy, and all Virginia Woolf audiobooks).
19. Saxophone holder (load distributed evenly with counterweights).
20. (Not pictured) Freeze-dried vegetarian entrées (indispensible when insensitive meat-eaters are put in charge of the school menu).

BART SIMPSON LISA'S OLDER NE'ER-DO-WELL BROTHER

Bart wants to have it all and usually gets what he wants, which is often more than he bargained for. Though Bart's mischief trumps Lisa's good behavior when it comes to parental attention, Lisa always helps him out in a pinch. She aids Bart in thwarting Sideshow Bob's diabolical schemes, shares his enjoyment of Itchy & Scratchy's murderous antics, and discovers zen in the art of miniature golf. For this, a grateful Bart demonstrates his appreciation with indifference, taunts, and an occasional surreptitious hug.

- **Quote:** "Lisa's got the brains and the talent to go as far as she wants, no matter what anyone says. And when she does, I'll be right there to borrow money."

- **First words:** Aye, Carumba!
- **Blood type:** Double-O negative.
- **Aliases:** Bartman, El Barto, Rudiger, and "the Boy."
- **Native American name:** Dances in Underwear.
- **Most heartwarming memory:** Roasting pinecones at Kamp Krusty.
- **Favorite ice cream:** Double Cappuccino Chocolate Chip.
- **Favorite beverage:** The syrupy goodness of a Kwik-E-Mart Squishee.
- **Heroes:** Krusty the Clown and Radioactive Man.
- **Secret desire:** To command an army of zombies.
- **Greatest fear:** That his good conscience might one day get the better of him.
- **Some notable achievements:** Has a comet named after him, taught a hamster to fly a miniature airplane, and synthesized a laxative from peas and carrots.

IF BART GOT HURT OR DIED, DESPITE THE EXTRA ATTENTION I'D RECEIVE, I'D MISS HIM.

With the Simpson family whirling and crashing around her, Maggie Simpson—blue-sleepered and adorable, with pacifier firmly in place—may well be indestructible. Having survived the questionable home remedies of doddering grandparents, Bart's rambunctious brothering, and Homer's hapless parenting, it is no wonder she feels most at home with animals—often sharing a waltz with Snowball II or a nourishing drink with Santa's Little Helper from his dog dish.

- **Nemesis:** Gerald, the baby with one eyebrow.
- **Head adornments:** Baseball cap, cowboy hat, coonskin cap, straw hat, hairnet, various bonnets, and the seemingly ever-present hair ribbon.
- **Semilethal weapons of choice:** Rifle, knife, rubber mallet, nail gun, circular saw, and pistol.
- **Favorite babysitters:** Snowball II, Santa's Little Helper, and bartender Moe Szyslak.
- **Musical talent:** Plays trumpet in the Simpson Family Mariachi Band and can perform "Dance of the Sugar Plum Fairy" on the xylophone.
- **Notable achievement:** Shot C. Montgomery Burns and once bowled a perfect game.
- **Sunscreen:** SPF 1000.
- **Favorite rides:** Santa's Little Helper, grizzly bears, and ceiling fans.
- **Likes:** Warm baths, pink elephant balloons, cheez from a can, and Balinese monkey chants.
- **Dislikes:** The philosophy of Ayn Rand and humoring idiotic people who make faces at her.
- **Greatest fear:** Being left in the tenderizing care of her aunts, Patty and Selma.

> MAGGIE IS A UNIQUE INDIVIDUAL. SHE DEFINITELY CRAWLS TO THE BEAT OF A DIFFERENT DRUM.

JANEY POWELL LISA SIMPSON'S FAIR-WEATHER BEST FRIEND

Janey Powell is widely considered one of the most popular girls in Springfield Elementary's second grade in a poll conducted by Janey Powell. She is very fashion conscious, being particularly wary of clothing that looks Canadian. Janey enjoys the company of other girls, especially when they are fawning. The way she sees it, you're either with her or you've got cooties.

- **Quote:** "We'd like to include you, but you just don't fit in."

- **Prized possession:** Never-ending Hair Malibu Stacy.
- **Sports:** Jumping rope, gossiping, and backbiting.
- **Favorite jump rope rhyme:** One plus one plus three is five. Little Bart Simpson's buried alive. He's so neat. He's so sweet. Now the rats have Bart to eat.
- **Special skill:** Can touch her nose with her tongue.
- **Hobby:** Calling boys and hanging up on them.
- **Turn-ons:** Pretty clothes, cute shoes, and all things Malibu Stacy.
- **Didja know:** Janey once scored a touchdown as a wide receiver on the Springfield Wildcats peewee football team.

The New Hampshire State Prison for Men makes license plates bearing the state's motto "Live Free or Die."

WITH FRIENDS LIKE HER, WHO NEEDS ACQUAINTANCES?

MILHOUSE VAN HOUTEN BART'S BEST FRIEND & LISA'S LOVELORN SUITOR

Despite his dalliances with Samantha Stanky and Greta Wolfcastle, Milhouse will forever carry a torch for Lisa Simpson. Milhouse's devotion to Lisa is such that once, while mourning her presumed death, he wanted to clone her from the spit in her saxophone. With his ultrathick glasses and low social standing, Milhouse seems like a nerd, but he's not. Nerds are smart. And, while unlucky in love, Milhouse is always able to score some pity from his mommy.

- **Quote:** "How could this happen? We started out like Romeo and Juliet, but it ended up in tragedy."

- **Medical prescriptions and conditions:** Takes Repressitol and is lactose intolerant.
- **Honorary title:** Class Clown Pro Tem (filling in for Bart).
- **Self-styled nickname:** Thrillhouse.
- **Secret shame:** Wimpier than Ralph Wiggum.
- **Personality traits:** Dogged, yet highly suggestible.
- **Likes:** Peruvian Fighting Frogs, luge silver medalist Barbara Niedernhuber, and the disturbing comfort of riding a girl's bike.
- **Dislikes:** Cooties, Smooshies, and scrunchies that get stuck in his hair.
- **Pastimes:** Sleepovers, collecting Great Place-kickers of the NFL model kits, and polishing feldspar in his rock tumbler.
- **Worships:** Krusty the Clown, Itchy & Scratchy, Carl Yastrzemski, and Lisa.
- **Member of:** The Cavalry Kids, the Hole in the Underwear Gang, and the Party Posse ("He's smart, he's soulful, he's Milhouse!").

I LIKE MILHOUSE A LOT. JUST NOT IN THAT WAY. HE'S MORE LIKE A BIG SISTER TO ME.

Though eight years old, Ralph Wiggum views the world with the innocent wonder of a newborn babe—with hygiene and social skills to match. So, naturally, his unabashed crush on Lisa causes her much embarrassment and ends badly. Yet despite his questionable physique, tangled English, and limited intellect, Ralph does have many amazing adventures—all imaginary.

- **Quote:** "I love Lisa Simpson, and when I grow up, I'm going to marry her."

- **Favorite book:** Go, Dog Go.
- **Favorite foods:** Popstickles, pudding, and paste.
- **Favorite swear word:** Mitten.
- **Musical instruments:** Bass drum and nose flute.
- **Special skills:** Puppy imitations, can consume and digest vast quantities of crayons, and can turn invisible by closing his eyes.
- **Aspirations:** To grow up to be either a principal or a caterpillar.
- **Future occupation:** Salmon gutter.
- **Closest friend:** Wiggle Puppy, an imaginary dog that flies by wagging its tail.
- **Lisa's valentine sentiment to Ralph:** "I Choo-Choo-Choose You."
- **Unfortunate circumstances:** Glued his head to his shoulder, got his tongue stuck in a finger trap, and bent his wookie.
- **Proud member of:** The Party Posse and the Pre-Teen Braves.
- **Sleep secret:** Requires plush novelty Reggie Rabbit and a blindingly bright nightlight.

I ONLY GAVE HIM A VALENTINE 'CAUSE I FELT SORRY FOR HIM.

The SuperFriends are a very select group of academically gifted students at Springfield Elementary, blessed with abilities beyond their years and, consequently, reviled by most other students. This does not mean they are ignored, however, for the SuperFriends are incredibly useful as human shields during spit-wad skirmishes, ready subjects for wedgie practice, and serve as valuable "friends" during standardized tests.

- **Quote:** "We are the SuperFriends!"

- **Identifying physical characteristics:**
  Ham: Wears suspenders and a red bow tie, thinning hair parted in the middle, and round wire-rimmed, coke-bottle glasses.
  Database: Black curly hair, round red glasses, top button of shirt always buttoned, and no tie.
  E-mail: Red wavy hair, receding chin, half-moon shaped glasses, suspenders, and bow tie.
  Cosine: Asian features, bowl-cut black hair, and long tie.
  Report Card: Indian features, black pompadour, blue tie, and pocket protector.
- **Nicknames:** Dr. Dorkmeister, Poindexter, Dweeb, Sir Nerdlinger, Brainiac, Brain Boy, Brainy Brain Boy, and Dumb Ass.
- **Motto:** "There's safety in numbers. And in hiding."
- **Hangouts:** Springfield Knowledgeum ("Where Science is Explained with Brightly Colored Balls"), The Android's Dungeon, and the Springfield lemon tree.
- **Organizational affiliations:** School band, school choir, chess club, The Junior Mathemagicians, and the Future Bachelors of America.

TECHNICALLY I BELONG TO THE SUPERFRIENDS, BUT I'M NOT SURE I WANT TO BE A PART OF ANY CLUB THAT WOULD HAVE ME AS A MEMBER.

Lisa's Guide to BEING A

- Volume counts! With a good thesaurus and a little imagination, you can turn a three-page assignment into a twelve-page assignment.

- Presentation is everything. Put your lunch money toward a leather portfolio to really put that book report over the top.

- Make yourself available for those essential but thankless tasks. Those erasers aren't going to clap themselves, you know.

- If possible, stop Ralph from licking the class lizard (my class only).

- Buy "World's Best Teacher" mugs in bulk for big savings.

- Today's ultra-convenient camera cell phones make tattling a snap and provide hard evidence to boot!

- Apples for teacher are strictly last century. Here's where gift certificates to Cinnabon and Starbucks come in handy.

- Offer to deliver homework to sick classmates.

- Be considerate! Try to whisper and tiptoe when the teacher's hung over.

TEACHER'S PET

- Sure, the other kids may laugh when you bring your own globe polish from home, but no teacher likes waxy, yellow build-up on her Madagascar!

- Helpfully remind the teacher when she forgets about a scheduled quiz. (Warning: Be discreet or expect multiple after school beatings from your classmates.)

- When making art from macaroni and glitter, introduce other types of pasta for variety. Capellini, rigatoni, and ziti will tell your teacher that you appreciate her assignment and that you don't see it as the pointless busy work that it really is.

- If possible, try to stop Ralph from eating the shavings from the pencil sharpener (again, my class only).

- Three words: footnotes, footnotes, footnotes!*

- Arrive early each day and confiscate practical jokes, comic books, and all forms of contraband from your classmates' desks.

- Competitive academics doesn't *have* to be a group effort. Why not have a solo spelling bee during free time?

- Create teacher factoid trading cards to collect and trade with other kids! (Look, if you get beat up for trying these ideas, it's your own fault for going outside at recess.)

- Make up a haiku using your teacher's name (the example below is my work, so *no copying*!).

Miss Hoover, sublime
Grade-giver, knowledge fountain,
Ralph, stop eating that!!

*and more footnotes!

Meet in Elementary School

The Knight in Shining Corduroy

The Jack Booted Thug

The Usual Suspect

The Tool of the System

The True Believer

The Doppelganger

The Flat Liner

The Idealist

The Drifter

Whatever

DR. LISA, VETERINARIAN TO THE STARS

TO BE CONTINUED...

Anatomy of Lisa

Maine is the only U.S. state whose name has just one syllable.

1. Nose – Sniffs out disturbing trends. **2. Brain** – Working overtime to release serotonin thanks to information gathered by her eyes, ears, nose. **3. Eyes** – Bright, shining windows into her oft-tortured soul. **4. Hair** – She can't do a thing with it, except pop balloons. **5. Smile** – Hiding years of intellectual disappointment. **6. Ears** – Sensitively attuned to hear each and every sour note and family squabble. **7. Books** – A little light reading: "Singularities in Homogeneous World Models" by Hawkings & Ellis, "Antologia" by Sylvia Plath. **8. Fingers** – Once deemed too stubby to ever belong to a great musician, they defy naysayers, let loose, and fly over her sax keys when pressed into service, like musical salmon defying currents and swimming upstream to spawn. **9. Feet** – Nimble, graceful; although never made for "tappa-tappa-tappa." **10. Dress** – She likes the design so much, she could wear it almost every day! **11. Stomach** – Over the teeth, past the gums, if it's meat, it shall not come. **12. Heart** – Goes out to all innocent creatures and liberal causes. **13. Arm** – Throws like a girl. **14. Saxophone** – Constant companion, her solace, friend, sense of identity; but not when Homer's watching TV. **15. Faux-pearl necklace** – White like her purity, cheap like her dad.

LISA'S LEFT BRAIN V

Pythagorean Theorem: $a^2 + b^2 = c^2$

Beethoven Symphony No. 7, 2nd Movement

Mon dieu! Quelle daube, cette chanson!

Krusty is a vulgar buffoon!

DNA sequencing

$C_6H_{12}O_6$

Herman Melville's *Moby-Dick*

Probability theory

The spiritual bankruptcy of consumerism

$(x \times y) \times z = x \times (y \times z)$

Darwin's *Origin of the Species*

Cogito, ergo sum: I think therefore I am.

The shortest distance between two points is a straight line.

In the early 20th century, the words "moron," "imbecile," and "idiot" were categories used to identify persons who scored low on IQ tests.

LISA'S RIGHT BRAIN

Veronica / Archie / Betty love triangle

The *Itchy & Scratchy* theme song

My God! What a crappy song!

Krusty is a comic genius!

Am I adopted?

Oh boy! Cupcakes!

Save the whales.

Bart did it!

Buy me that!

No matter how you slice it, it's still baloney.

I ♥ UNICORNS

My imaginary friend Rachel Cohen

Are we there yet?

In 1951, "Newsweek" reported the term "nerd" being used in Detroit, Michigan, to describe a "drip" or a "square."

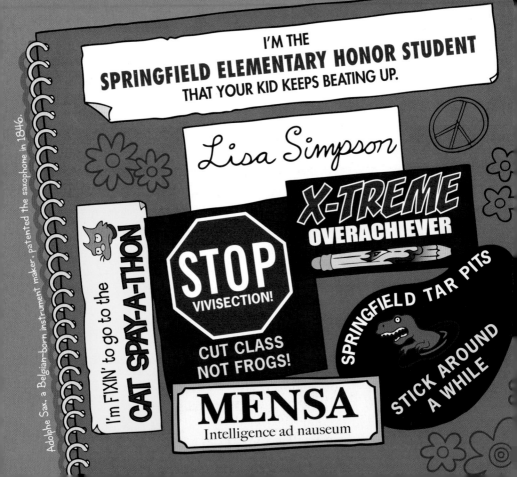

Lisa Simpson's
DVD Shelf

THE LITTLE LOCOMOTIVE THAT TRIED BUT FAILED

Who Feeds Ya, Baby? The Telly Savalas Tubbies

THE COMPLETE ITCHY & SCRATCHY MASTERPIECE EDITION

I Only Have Ping-Pong Balls for You *A Muppets Love Story*

The Day the Plastic Maxed Out the Lip Gloss Girls Christmas Special

Pretentious Art House Presents: Jane Austen LIVE!

RE-RUNS FOR WEE ONES   VOL. XXVIII

L' Enfant Einstein: A DIAPER FULL OF THEORIES

National Wildlife's Big Box of Beasts

SWEDE CHARITY Ye Olde Sven Twins

THE PACK RATS COLLECTOR'S COLLECTION

There's a list of all 50 states running across the top of the Lincoln Memorial on the back of a $5 bill.

DR. LISA, VETERINARIAN TO THE STARS

TO BE CONTINUED...

The Case of the Cold-Cocked Clown

A MINI-MYSTERY FROM
THE SECRET FILES OF LISA SIMPSON

Krusty the Clown was out like a light. The hapless harlequin was slumped in a chair across from his desk, a black and blue beauty of a bump rising off his forehead. An empty bottle of whiskey lay on its side on the carpet behind the desk.

"Looks like it's curtains for Krusty the Clown…well, at least for tonight!" said Chief Clancy Wiggum, standing next to the insensate entertainer with Officer Lou. "After all, the show must go on!" said the police chief, referring to Krusty's bone-headed second banana who was frantically performing that afternoon's show single-handed.

I sat in the audience next to my brother Bart, watching flop sweat pour off of Sideshow Mel's forehead as he capered about the stage. First came the desperate sidekick's unrehearsed opening monologue with rushed setups and badly timed punchlines, and then the "surefire" cream pie to the puss went off half-cocked when Mel shoved the pastry in his own face. Krusty's two-man act was suddenly a single. Bart didn't notice me leave the studio in search of answers. I gave two cameramen and one production assistant the slip and made my way into the wings to find out what happened to Krusty.

"Lookee here, Lou, if it isn't little Lisa Simpson." I couldn't help but notice the sarcasm in Chief Wiggum's voice. "Just what we need, a pint-sized shamus putting out her shingle at my crime scene."

"Good one, Chief," said Officer Lou.

"As soon as Sideshow Mel gets off the stage," the police chief continued, "I'm booking him on a 327: Assault and Battery."

"You mean a 240, Chief," corrected Officer Lou. "A 327 is an illegal chain letter."

"But why do you suspect foul play, Chief Wiggum?" I asked.

"Take a look at that bump on Krusty's noggin. Isn't it obvious? That slidehorn-tootin' wannabe has been waiting in the wings for his time in the spotlight, and today he decided to take over the show by conking Krusty over the head with that whiskey bottle," deduced the chief. "I've got a nice warm jail cell just waiting for him. It's got a brand new space heater, and the bunk has a fresh set of flannel sheets. Yep…that's one cozy cell."

Krusty's assistant, Miss Pennycandy, rushed into the office, administered a cold compress to her boss's forehead, and massaged two extra-strength pain relievers down his throat. Any other detective might stop to notice the buxom Girl Friday had gams that stretched from Saturday to Monday like a three-day weekend, but I wasn't any other detective. I was only eight years old…and also a girl.

"Excuse me, Miss Pennycandy…did anyone come to see Krusty before the show?" I asked.

"Yes. Roger Meyers Jr. was here negotiating a new contract for the Itchy & Scratchy cartoons Krusty runs on his show. Mr. Meyers brought that bottle of whiskey as a peace offering, but pretty soon I heard yelling and screaming coming from the office…as usual. A little bit later, I heard the door slam and then there was a loud crash. I was on the phone with the network at the time. One thing led to another, and I forgot to check on Krusty. I didn't see Mr. Meyers leave," Miss Pennycandy explained.

Miss Pennycandy looked down at the floor. "Hmm…what's that stain doing on the carpet by the door? I cleaned up Krusty's office this morning, and I never saw that!"

"You heard the lady. It looks like the cartoon guy is the culprit," determined Wiggum. "Bring Meyers in and throw him in the hoosegow, Lou."

Krusty was comatose. Down for the count. Out cold. All I needed to do was let the who, what, where, and why fall into place. Then, with one glance downward, the how hit me, and I knew who had cleaned Krusty's clock.

"Not so fast, Chief Wiggum," I declared. "You've got the wrong man."

Can you solve the crime?
Look for Lisa's solution to "The Case of the
Cold-Cocked Clown" later in the book.

LISA'S SMART-ALECKY ANSWERS TO ENVIRONMENTALLY INSENSITIVE QUESTIONS

A highly-gifted student, Allison Taylor, supplants Lisa Simpson's reign as "Brain Queen" of the schoolyard by being better than Lisa at everything that makes Lisa special. She is a whiz at history and English, and she converses well above a normal eight-year-old level. As a result, she enjoys all the queenly schoolyard privileges—including the privilege of being pushed face first into a mud puddle.

- **Quote:** "I'm actually kinda glad I lost. Now I know losing isn't the end of the world."

- **Schoolyard nicknames:** "Brainiac," "Nerd," and "Geekazoid."
- **First impression:** Made Miss Hoover go "Yowie!"
- **Identifying markers:** Ever-present hair band and necklace.
- **Sports:** Gymnastics, darts, and tap dancing.
- **Dance instructor:** Little Vicki Valentine.
- **Favorite game:** Anagrams—take a proper name and rearrange the letters to form a description of that person.
- **Bedroom decor:** Walls lined with highly polished trophies, plaques, and medals.
- **Allison's diorama:** "The Tell-Tale Heart" by Edgar Allan Poe

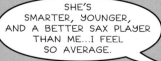

SHE'S SMARTER, YOUNGER, AND A BETTER SAX PLAYER THAN ME...I FEEL SO AVERAGE.

Poised, confident, and ultracute, Amber Dempsey is a force to be reckoned with in the Little Miss beauty pageant circuit. Her eyelashes alone, which she bats with an almost lethal precision, make her nearly unbeatable, but she is also well versed in the other tricks of the trade: taping your swimsuit to your butt, putting petroleum jelly on your teeth for that frictionless smile, and the ancient art of padding.

- **Quote:** "My name is Amber Dempsey, and when I grow up, I want to be a sweetie pie."

- **Hair:** Blonde, curly, luxuriant—tiara worthy.
- **Eyelashes:** Implants, procured in Paraguay.
- **Smile:** Dazzling.
- **Dress:** Fur-trimmed coat, sequined sailor suit, blue shoes, frilly socks, pink hair bow, and blue shades.
- **Her other titles:** Simultaneously held crowns as Pork Princess and Little Miss Kosher; later named Little Miss Intensive Care.
- **Word to the wise:** If you're gonna binge, you'd better purge.
- **Winner's routine:** Gasp, wipe away a tear, hug the loser, and walk triumphantly down the runway.
- **Little Miss Springfield's responsibilities:** Attending football games, entertaining the troops at Fort Springfield with Bob Hope, bidding farewell to deportees, and turning on the "Severe Tire Damage" spikes at store openings.
- **Pageant location:** Ye Olde Off-Ramp Inn ("We're Now Rat-Free!")

THERE'S NO WAY I CAN BEAT THIS GIRL. SHE'S THE JACK NICKLAUS OF THE PAGEANT CIRCUIT.

Ultrahip and condescending, Alex Whitney makes Lisa feel like a little baby. Alex has an outfit for every occasion and seizes on any occasion to show off her outfits. She loves to fabulize herself with makeup, lip gloss, perfume, and platform shoes. While Alex Whitney might appear too cool for school, her weakness for a good greaseball fight always wins out in the end.

- **Quote:** "Oh yeah, like I'd be seen with a Discover card."

- **Favorite scent:** Calvin Klein's Pretension.
- **Favorite drink:** Iced tea.
- **Favorite store:** Dingo Junction.
- **Favorite putdown:** "Don't be such a Phoebe!"
- **Status symbols:** Cell phone, purse, and credit card.
- **Ear-piercing equipment:** Thumbtacks and a whole lot of paper towels.
- **Likes:** Shopping on credit, dating, and fuzzy pink backpacks.
- **Dislikes:** Playing hopscotch, baking cookies, and "The McLaughlin Group."
- **Catch phrases:** "Shut-up," "Helloo?," "No doubt," "What's the haps?," and "DMY," which means "Don't mess yourself." Duhhh!
- **Breaking news:** The new Malibu Stacy has an achievable chest.

The four most common elements in the universe are hydrogen, helium, oxygen, and ignorance.

THE OTHER GIRLS ARE ALREADY INTO FASHION AND MAKEUP AND DATING. THEY MAKE ME FEEL LIKE A LITTLE BABY.

Initially, Lisa thinks new student Francine is shy and lonely. But when Lisa tries to befriend her and is punched out, Francine's true colors are revealed. She is a skilled practitioner of the art of bullying, a time-honored pastime that even predates agriculture. Francine enjoys punching, tripping, shoving, hogging the teeter-totter, knocking heads, imprisoning people in lockers, and biting the heads off Malibu Stacy dolls.

- **Quote:** "Suck fist, Dr. Dork!"

- **Hair:** Red.
- **Build:** Stocky and strong.
- **Demeanor:** Forbidding.
- **Speech:** Monosyllabic.
- **Dress:** Frilly white shirt, blue jumper, pink socks, and pink hair bow.
- **Shoes:** Canadian looking.
- **Prized possession:** Green plaid lunch box.
- **Dislikes:** Geeks, nerds, and brainiacs.
- **Likes:** Beating up geeks, nerds, and brainiacs.
- **Best punch:** Right cross.
- **Special skill:** Triple twist Indian burn administered by hand.
- **The key to bully/nerd antagonism:** Nerd sweat.
- **Partial victims list:** Lisa, Milhouse, Ralph Wiggum, Database, Martin Prince, Prof. Frink, former United States surgeon general Dr. C. Everett Koop, and the guy who invented the walkie-talkie.

I FINALLY DISCOVERED WHY THE BRAWNY PICK ON THE BRAINY. I ISOLATED THE CHEMICAL THAT IS EMITTED BY EVERY GEEK, DORK, AND FOUR-EYES. I CALL IT "POINDEXTROSE."

A Cautionary Guide to the

MISS MEAN TEEN U.S.A.

Most marked characteristic: Propensity for violence

Marketing slogan: Super Psycho Action Figure

WHATSERNAME

Most marked characteristic: None

Marketing slogan: Bland Is Beautiful

MALIBU STACY

Most marked characteristic: Sexist stereotype

Marketing slogan: America's Favorite 8½-Incher

PRINCESS PHONEY

Most marked characteristic: Doubles as a cell phone

Marketing slogan: The Multi-Tasking Toy for Busy Little Girls

POLLY PROPYLENE

Most marked characteristic: $(C_3H_6)_x$

Marketing slogan: She's Thermoplastic Fantastic!

WORST DOLLS EVER!

G.I. JENNIFER
*Most marked
characteristic:
Fashionable
under fire*

*Marketing
slogan:
An Army of One
Adorable Doll*

CLINGY CLEO
*Most marked
characteristic:
Pathological
attachment
(Velcro)*

*Marketing
slogan:
The Only REAL
Friend You'll
Ever Have*

LI'L BELLE LEMIA
*Most marked
characteristic:
Binging and
purging*

*Marketing
slogan:
She Eats!
She Pukes!*

GENEVA THE JUNKIE
SUPER MODEL
*Most marked
characteristic:
Self-destruction*

*Marketing
slogan:
Très Chic!*

MALL TILDA
*Most marked
characteristic:
Obsessive
accessorizing*

*Marketing
slogan:
A Lifetime of
Compulsive
Shopping Begins
Here!*

Up On My High

Lisa Simpson's Blogosphere of News and Opinions...But Mostly Opinions

HOT TOPICS

A Very Special Television Event!
Corey Masterson is slated to star as Corey Cassidy in *Born Too Cute: The Corey Story*.
READ / POST COMMENTS (1)

The Springfield Elementary School Cafeteria Announces Tofu Tuesdays!
READ / POST COMMENTS (3)

New Bunsen Burners Heat Up Science Fair Competition
READ / POST COMMENTS (1)

PET PEEVES

Whacking Day
There is no excuse for beating snakes with clubs...unless you count beating snakes instead of beating the Irish as an excuse, but then that's hardly an excuse, now is it?
READ / POST COMMENTS (2)

Rant Radio
Just for one blissful moment, imagine a world without that bombastic blowhard Birch Barlow in it...
READ / POST COMMENTS (0)

Sibling Misery
Ever since Cain slew Abel, brothers have been an unending source of human suffering...
> CLICK HERE TO VIEW TO WHOM I AM REFERRING

THE VIEW FROM GRADE 2

Why am I still wasting away in here instead of being skipped ahead?
READ / POST COMMENTS (0)

What does Miss Hoover know that she's NOT teaching us?
READ / POST COMMENTS (2)

With friends like these who needs enemies?
> CLICK HERE FOR COMPLETE LIST

ALL THINGS COREY

High Horse Music Review:
The Many Moods of Corey
On TV This Week:
"Born Too Cute: The Corey Story"
Corey in Concert Review:
IT'S LIKE A SCREAM COME TRUE!!!
Corey Hotline FAQ.

TAKE ACTION!

Tell Congress to vote themselves a pay cut.

> Click here for more good ideas like this.

Horse

SEARCH

Pull Down for Peeves

THE LISA ALERT

Up-to-the-Minute Emails
of My Musings and Epiphanies
> SIGN UP

IRKSOME ISSUES

Just when I thought they couldn't sink any lower, Laramie Cigarettes introduces a new ad campaign featuring Rachel the Chain-smoking Raccoon...
READ / POST COMMENTS (0)

Surely I am not the only one who finds static cling annoying…
READ / POST COMMENTS (9)

Why is it that Bart is the only one who posts comments on my site? And why are your comments so idiotic, Bart?
READ / POST COMMENTS (36)

All right, Bart. Knock it off.
READ / POST COMMENTS (87)

I mean it, Bart!
READ / POST COMMENTS (648)

THIS JUST IN

Springfield Dethroned as "America's Crappiest City"…

Study Shows Smart Kids Don't Smell Any Different Than Anybody Else…

My Dad Ate the Last Two Cookies That Mom Was Saving for My Lunch Tomorrow…

New Research Indicates Children Who Own Ponies Grow Up Healthier, Happier…

LINKS BY CATEGORY
- Truth Seekers
- Zero Emissions
- Bleeding Gums Murphy Fansites
- Recycled Compostings
- All Things Itchy & Scratchy
- Beboppin' Blogs
- Krusty Korners
- The Happy Little Elves Free Downloads

SEARCH THE ARCHIVES
- My Poems about Mr. Bergstrom
- My Complaints about Bart
- Things My Dad Did That Totally Embarrassed Me
- Insults Hurled at Me
- My Rebuttals
- My Apologies
- What I Had for Dinner Last Night

JUST WHINING
- I'm Bored
- There's Nothing on TV
- I Hate Baloney
- My Foot's Asleep
- Bart Won't Shut Up
- I Can't Find My Mittens
- It's Stuffy in Here
- Someone Ate My Cupcake
- I Think I'm Getting Carpal Tunnel Syndrome

LISA'S BOOKSHELF

Darby O'Dirty - The Despicable, Disgusting, Distasteful Little Troll
>LEARN MORE
A Short War and Then Some Peace
A Reading Digest Boiled-Down Book
>LEARN MORE

TODAY'S POLL

Should Mayor Quimby be impeached?

O Yes, he should!
O No, he should not!!
O Maybe, I don't know!!!

>VOTE NOW

ILLUSTRATED MAP OF WASHINGTON, D.C.

Ponies are not baby horses. They are breeds of horses that are small in size when full-grown. They do not grow up to be big horses.

OUR NATION'S CAPITAL

GERRY MANDER'S HOMESTYLE BUFFET

1. The White House
2. Special Interests Executive Office Building
3. Monument to the Unknown Crony
4. Washington Lobbyists' Lobby and Foyer
5. The Public Trough
6. Ye Olde Flag-on-a-Stick Gift Shoppe
7. National Archives of Shame
8. Richard M. Nixon Center for the Perfidious Arts
9. Almighty Dollar Ministries
10. National Shooting Gallery
11. Final Resting Place of Liberty
12. Ronald Reagan Hair Club for Men
13. First Church of Bad Faith
14. The Cradle of Jingoism
15. International House of Bamboozle Restaurant
16. Tomb of Reasonable Dialogue
17. Gerry Mander's Homestyle Buffet
18. Roamin' Senate
19. House of Misrepresentatives
20. Pork Barrel Rotunda
21. Library of Deleted Passages
22. J. Edgar Hoover's Fancy Dress Museum
23. Benedict Arnold's Bistro & Gallery of Treason
24. Church of Close Personal Friends of Jesus Christ
25. The Gridlock Society
26. JFK's Brain-in-a-Jar
27. Homeland Security Survival Supply Strip Mall
28. Islamic Jihad Recruitment Center (located upstairs
    from Department of Homeland Security)
29. Bill Clinton Memorial Humidor
30. Natural His & Herstory Museum
31. Chester A. Arthur Souvenir Kiosk
32. U.S.S. Weak Constitution—"Old Gushy Guts"
33. Culture War Memorial
34. Logrollers Saloon
35. The Washington Monument
36. Statue of Limitations
37. The Lincoln Memorial
38. Temple Beth Goyim
39. ACLU Museum of Selective Tolerance
40. Boondoggle's Bar & Grill

This Sash I Wear THE HALL MONITOR'S PLEDGE

DON'T HATE ME BECAUSE I'M SNITCHIFUL!

PUMA PRIDE

I, Lisa Simpson, do solemnly vow to guard and protect the hallowed halls of my school, despite whatever adversity my oath of office may bring.

No running shall be permitted. No loud chatter shall go unchecked. No locker shall be adorned with Krusty pinups or Silly String or derogatory cartoons of our principal or teachers while I am at my post. Vigilance, dedication, and pink slips—these are my weapons in the war against the vicious and relentless spread of tardiness and tomfoolery:

When a student doth abuse his temporary bathroom pass, I will be there; When a truant doth hazard to arrive without a proper written excuse, be it doctor's note or parent and/or guardian letter from home, mine eyes will be the eyes that do glare MOST disapprovingly;

When between class snacking doth occur, I will be the stern voice of authority, stating equivocally for all the world to hear, "No eatsies 'til lunch;" And when anyone doth attempt "cuts" in the milk line, I will be the sole firewall against the chaos of the dreaded "grab 'n' gulp."

No exceptions, no spitwads, no friends—this is the credo of the bearer and wearer of this noble sash.

I am not merely the officer of the law in these corridors; I am also a friend to those in need:

When a foreign exchange student doth receive an uber-wedgie, it is I who will dry his tears; When a bathroom doth need additional "rolls," it is I who will fetch Groundskeeper Willie before a single classmate is left "behind;" And when a good day's education is threatened by the scourge of good-natured fun, it is I who will stand straight and tall and proudly exclaim, "The bell is about to ring."

I do not expect to be thanked. My reward is the unspoken gratitude in the eyes of each of my fellow students (I am pretty sure that it is unspoken gratitude and not unspoken resentment) for me, my position, and my school.

For I am a HALL MONITOR.

Also, I get extra credit.

DR. LISA, VETERINARIAN TO THE STARS

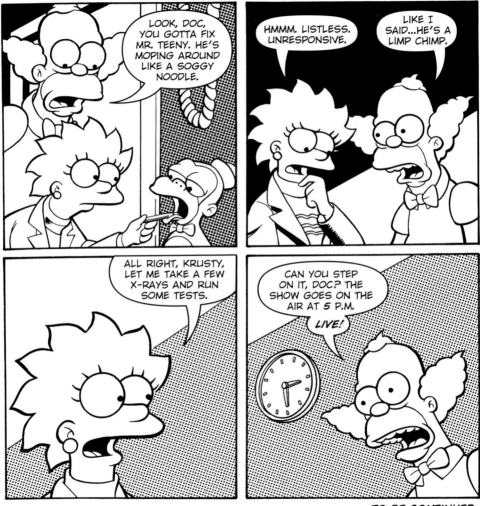

TO BE CONTINUED...

FREELOADING

BACK STABBING

MONEY GRUBBING

WAFFLING

COUCH POTATO

FISHING FOR COMPLIMENTS

BAD SPORTSMANSHIP

BACKSEAT DRIVING

BACK PEDALING

BROWNNOSING

WHISTLE BLOWING

FLIP-FLOPPING

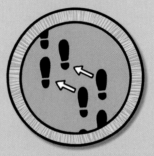

SIDESTEPPING

PENCIL PUSHING

FOOT DRAGGING

ASS COVERAGE

RUMOR MONGERING

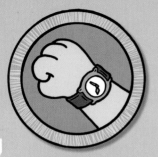

CLOCK WATCHING

PROMISE BREAKERS OF AMERICA

BUTT KISSING

RUBBERNECKING

WHITEWASHING

BOOT LICKING

ONE-UPSMANSHIP

CHEAPSKATERY

HORSE'S ASSMANSHIP

Lisa Simpson's Sure-Fire, All-Purpose, Feeble Yet Effective, Excuses for Getting Out of Gym Class

- I am suffering from Athlete's Block.
- I left my defibrillator at home.
- I'm a devout anti-recreationist.
- My right kidney is on the fritz.
- I have a hangnail.
- The gym is built on an ancient Indian burial ground.
- My arches have fallen, and I can't get up.
- I wish to exercise my right not to exercise.
- My get up and go got up and went.
- My therapist says getting picked last for teams has irreparably damaged my self-esteem.
- My kneecap is swollen from my nightly prayers for more school gym funds.
- The maharishi advises retreat from the physical world.
- I threw my back out doing mental gymnastics.
- I have Tennis Elbow, Swimmer's Ear, Housemaid's Knee, and Athlete's Foot.
- The bench needs warming.
- My religious beliefs do not permit me to engage in self-gratifying competition.
   - I can't afford to be smarter AND in better shape than the rest of my family. I'll never hear the end of it.
   - When the going gets tough, I get tachycardia.

No new animals have been domesticated in the last 4,000 years. However, most species have been reduced to anthropomorphic idiocy through computer-generated imagery.

DR. LISA, VETERINARIAN TO THE STARS

TO BE CONTINUED...

NELSON MUNTZ BULLY AND UNEXPECTED LOVE INTEREST

In a wild swing away from the nonthreatening boys she is usually smitten with, Lisa fell for the undeniably threatening Nelson Muntz. Despite appearances, she thought there was a sweet sensitive person inside Nelson.

At first, Nelson went along with Lisa's attempt to reform him, getting a new haircut and outfit at "Wee Monsieur." Eventually, however, he assured her that what's really inside him is guts and black stuff and about fifty Slim Jims.

- **Quote:** "Okay, Lisa. I'll come over to your house. But if anybody sees us, I'm just there to steal your bike."

- **Weapon of choice:** Killmatic 3000.
- **Musical instrument:** Harmonica.
- **Favorite songs:** "Little Brown Jug" and anything sung by Andy Williams.
- **Posters in his room:** Nuke the Whales, Bomb the Arabs and Take Their Oil, Bomb the Indians and Take Their Casinos.
- **Likes:** Huckleberries, ice cream, fried carrots, and Snow White.
- **Dislikes:** Sissy wimps, Space Camp simulators, and authority figures.
- **Affiliations:** Pre-Teen Braves, Party Posse ("He'll break your nose, your glasses, and your heart"), quarterback for the Springfield Wildcats, and claims to be part Eskimo.
- **Partial list of items hucked:** Beehives, rocks, mud, fish, snowballs, grease balls, tiny dogs, shoes, rotten tomatoes, Bart Simpson, and expired coleslaw.
- **His cartoon creation:** Danger Cat.
- **Fondest dream:** To one day see Macon, Georgia.
- **Secret shame:** Proficient in Home Economics class.

> HE'S NOT LIKE ANYBODY I'VE EVER MET. HE'S LIKE A RIDDLE WRAPPED IN AN ENIGMA WRAPPED IN A VEST. OH NO! I THINK I'M GETTING A CRUSH ON NELSON MUNTZ!

With his bravery, nonthreatening Bobby Sherman-style good looks, and holier-than-thou environmental ideals, eco-hunk Jesse Grass captivates Lisa Simpson's heart and mind. Over the course of his anticorporate crusade, Jesse has been imprisoned repeatedly, hosed down with Tabasco sauce, and been shot off a roof while dressed up like a cow. Despite these privations, he firmly believes that you can't silence the truth with beanbags and that one day he will acquire super powers.

- **Quote:** "I'm a level-5 vegan. I won't eat anything that casts a shadow."

- **Hair:** Blond and dreadlocked.
- **Dress:** Tattered blue pants, brown hoody, and waffle stompers.
- **Appearance:** Cute and committed.
- **Characteristic pose:** Upraised clenched fist.
- **Protest slogans:** "Krusty Burger = Earth Murder," and "Take Down the Clown."
- **Preferred mode of transport:** Bicycle.
- **Likes:** Yoga, Phish concerts, solar power, pocket mulching, and Burning Man.
- **Dislikes:** The St. Patrick's Day Parade, secret tree-auctions, Krusty Burger, nonsolar-powered electric chairs, and redwoods used as promotional tools.

HIS IDEALISM AND BRAVERY INSPIRE ME ALMOST AS MUCH AS HIS DREAMY EYES AND DREADLOCKED GOOD LOOKS.

LUKE STETSON JUNIOR WRANGLER, LAZY "I" DUDE RANCH

On a vacation at the Lazy "I" Dude Ranch (formerly the Wandering "I" Nudist Colony), Lisa meets and falls for Luke Stetson. Environmentally aware and sensitive to animal rights, Luke teaches Lisa about the New West, where both equine and bovine Americans are respected. He rescues a rattlesnake egg and shows Lisa how to ride a horse. Later, they make beautiful music in the moonlight (Luke on guitar and Lisa on sax).

- **Quote:** "I need somebody to help me hang these 'No Hunting' and 'Free Tibet' signs."

  - **Age:** 13.
  - **Hair:** Blond.
  - **Looks:** Rugged, in a sensitive, nonthreatening way.
  - **Favorite color:** Blue—just like the wide open western sky.
  - **Musical instrument:** Acoustic guitar.
  - **Likes:** Cloud gazing, square dancing, and serenades under the stars.
  - **Dislikes:** City slickers with a lot of chutzpah.
  - **Lazy "I" Dude Ranch motto:** "Peace. Quiet. Chili."
  - **Alternate vacation options:** The Denzel Washington Monument, Colonial Phoenix, and Walter Gropius' Bauhaus Village.

I HAD MY FIRST CRUSH, AND ALL IT DID WAS MAKE ME DO TERRIBLE THINGS AND THEN BREAK MY HEART.

Brilliant, refined, Englishman Hugh Parkfield meets Lisa Simpson in the library of an eastern American university in 2010. Like Lisa, Hugh is studying the environment, is utterly humorless about his vegetarianism, and loves the Rolling Stones (not for their music but for their tireless efforts to preserve historic buildings). They fall in love, but unfortunately, it ends badly.

- **Quote:** "You know, I've attempted to enjoy your family on a personal level, on an ironic level, as a novelty, as camp, as kitsch, as cautionary example—nothing works."

- **Residence:** Parkfield Manor.
- **Student residence:** Dr. & Mrs. Dre Hall.
- **Hair:** Thick, luxuriant, and always well kept.
- **Dress:** Tasteful and tradition-bound, favoring open-collared dress shirts and sweater vests.
- **Accent:** Received Standard English.
- **Preferred snack:** Soy Pop "Now with Gag Suppressant."
- **Reading skills:** Above a 78th grade level.
- **Book that brought Hugh and Lisa together:** "Ecosystem of the Marsh" by Thompson.
- **First date:** "Ace Ventura VI" at the 40 Classic Films of Jim Carrey Festival.
- **Wedding plans:** Springfield Meadow, Sunday, One P.M., August 1, 2010.
- **Didja know:** In the future when robots cry, they short circuit, and then their heads burst into flame and melt.

I MAY COMPLAIN ABOUT MY FAMILY MORE THAN ANYONE, BUT I STILL LOVE THEM, AND I DON'T THINK HE UNDERSTANDS THAT.

A Typical Day in the Life

6:00 a.m. - Friday morning. Up at crack of dawn, not only to practice Buddhist meditations, but also to get into bathroom before Bart.

6:25 a.m. - Barely reaches bathroom before Bart. Grappling/hand slapping/noogies ensue.

7:00 a.m. - Pours pitcher of orange juice out bedroom window sending libations to Mother Earth.

7:00 a.m. - Milhouse, having come to serenade her beneath her bedroom window, is drenched with orange juice/runs home crying in wet Romeo costume.

7:30 a.m. - Eats peach-sweetened grits for breakfast/debates with Homer whether invention of sliced bread is really that great.

7:45 a.m. - Marge comments on how much orange juice family consumes/makes Lisa's vegetarian lunch, sneaking small amount of beef juice into macaroni salad "for Lisa's own good."

8:00 a.m. - School bus arrives. Once outside, Lisa tosses beef juice-laced macaroni salad into garbage/replaces it with nontainted macaroni salad she smuggled out of house.

8:05 a.m. - During bus ride, distributes flyers for downtown "Leave Trees Be" rally, printed on recycled hemp stationery purchased with own money. Most kids make airplanes out of flyers/throw them at her.

8:30 a.m. - At school before class, Milhouse tries to attract her attention by winking (technique he learned from one of his dad's men's magazines).

8:31 a.m. - Lisa does not pay attention to Milhouse. He winks so much, he accidentally trips/falls into wasp nest behind bushes.

# of Lisa Simpson

8:35 a.m. - History lesson. Lisa wonders aloud why class cannot study socio-economic pitfalls of Greco-Roman Empire/its relation to modern G8 world. Miss Hoover takes first "headache" pill of day.

9:15 a.m. - Science lesson. Screams in horror when Ralph Wiggum shows her "biology of booger" on his finger, up close/personal. Miss Hoover takes two more "headache" pills.

10:00 a.m. - Math lesson. Tries to point out mistakes she found in Teacher's Version of math textbook. Miss Hoover falls asleep.

10:30 a.m. - Recess. With bullhorn borrowed from gym teacher, attempts to rally support for her student council "Swirlies Waste Water" amendment.

10:31 a.m. - Any hope for amendment support vanishes when moaning Milhouse emerges from nurse's office, wrapped head-to-toe in bandages from wasp stings. "The Mummy!" students cry, running away.

11:00 a.m. - Music lesson. Interrupts band's mediocre rendition of "Stars and Stripes Forever," adding mad Sonny Rollins-style riffs on saxophone. As usual, told to take it outside.

11:45 a.m. - Lunchtime. Eats at principal's desk while Principal Skinner is out monitoring cafeteria. Uses phone to repeatedly harass local congressman about tragic plight of baby chicks shipped in mail.

12:28 p.m. - As lunchtime ends, Milhouse tries to talk to her, managing only to hobble/mumble/ fall through door Groundskeeper Willie left open leading downstairs into basement. (Milhouse spends entire weekend there.)

12:35 p.m. - Art lesson. Miss Hoover asks Lisa to take over class, claiming she had "tee many martoonies" during lunch.

12:45 p.m. - Helps Ralph remove modeling clay stuck in his ears. Miss Hoover giggles incessantly.

1:15 p.m. - Language lesson. Since Miss Hoover is flirting with mailman, Lisa continues teaching class.

1:20 p.m. - Reads poem "Hospital Window" by Allen Ginsberg with sincere dramatic interpretation, subtly altering provocative parts.

1:23 p.m. - Disappointed when she lowers poetry book to find entire class snickering at Janey Powell imitating her in pantomime.

1:24 p.m. - Spends rest of class softly playing sax to self in corner.

2:10 p.m. - School's out! Passes principal's office as Superintendent Chalmers yells something about nagging phone calls to his congressman cousin. Skinner's eyes have taken on 'Nam flashback glaze.

2:15 p.m. - On bus ride home, converses with Otto about interesting advances in molecular biology/genetic sequence databases of agricultural research. He thinks she is talking about dudes who make LSD in bathtubs.

2:30 p.m. - Has afternoon snack while Bart wastes time trying to bend spoon with his mind. (Apparently, Milhouse is M.I.A.)

2:45 p.m. - Rides bike to Springfield Library, where she helps out every day after school shushing people.

3:45 p.m. - Rides to nearby field/picks flowers/weaves them into wreath for hair.

4:01 p.m. - Building contractor/steam shovel operators pitch fit because they cannot clear field for new Try-N-Save because "one goody-two-shoes little protester won't move."

4:30 p.m. - Relieved by fellow "Save Springfield's Field" activists, Seth and Munchie.

SAVE SPRINGFIELD'S FIELD

LIL' AGITATOR

111,111,111 × 111,111,111 = 12,345,678,987,654,321

4:31 p.m. - After Lisa's gone, construction workers beat up Seth and Munchie/start digging.

5:00 p.m. - Back at home. Bart is so bored, he agrees to do weekend homework early with Lisa.

5:07 p.m. - Lisa finishes homework. Bart finishes sharpening pencil.

5:10 p.m. - Sorts/alphabetizes Malibu Stacy outfits by designer.

6:00 p.m. - Dinner time. Fish sticks for everyone but Lisa, who lectures on evils of farmed fish until Marge silences her with a "Hrmmm."

6:45 p.m. - Friday night is movie night. Simpsons head for Googolplex—this week it is Lisa's pick. Lisa's choice (*Pride & Prejudice*) elicits duet of groans in car.

7:00 p.m. - Quick stop to drop off Maggie at aunts' apartment. Lisa pulls out a *Time* magazine clipping entitled "Spinsterhood & Cigarettes May Lead to Lonely Painful Death." Lisa quickly hustled out of apartment/down elevator/into car by aunts.

7:30 p.m. - Movie begins. Lisa cannot decide which is more embarrassing: Bart shooting popcorn out of his nose at screen/Homer loudly asking which character is Pride and which is Prejudice.

9:30 p.m. - Sleepy Lisa—headstrong feminist, political activist, Mensa member—still loves it when Daddy carries her into house from car.

9:45 p.m. - Time for one last smooth jazz sax solo, while sitting on windowsill/watching as late quarter moon rises over hills. Bart in his bed/Marge in her kitchen/Homer on his couch—all have same thought: "When is she going to cut out that racket and go to bed!"

10:00 p.m. - She ends her song and turns out the light.

DR. LISA, VETERINARIAN TO THE STARS

TO BE CONTINUED...

Lisa's Solution to "The Case of the Cold-Cocked Clown"

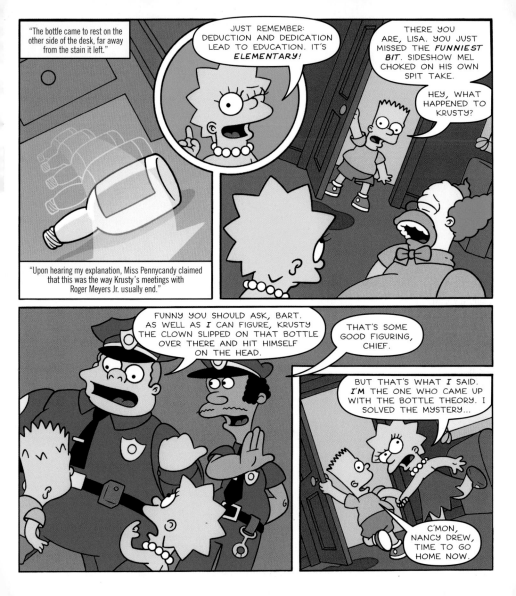

Lisa's House of Haiku

I am middle child,
And attention must be paid!
Uh, hello? Hello?

Bleeding Gums Murphy
Lives on in the summer wind.
Blow, Daddy-o, blow!

O, Mister Bergstrom!
There's no substitute for love,
My Jewish cowboy.

On a snowy night,
While stopping by the woods, please,
Hug a tree for me.

What's it like to be
The smartest one in the room?
Alone. So alone.

Happy Little Elves,
If you grow, you may not be
Happy, little elves.

In German folklore, elves are believed to bring bad dreams to sleepers; hence, the German word for nightmare, "albtraum," means "elf dream."

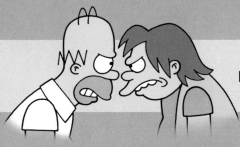

First crush. Nelson Muntz.
Dimwitted. Lowbrow. Apelike.
Daddy, is that you?

What's that peculiar
Odor in geeks, dorks, and nerds?
Poindextrose, dummy!

Without irony,
Does thinking give you wrinkles,
Malibu Stacy?

mensa
Stacy

SPRINGFIELD
TIRE FIRE
NOW SMELLED
IN 46 STATES

A burning tire dump
Lights the petrol-scented sky.
That smell? It's Springfield!

Gazpacho. Tofu.
Bunly dogless hot dog bun.
Vegetarian.

THERE IS NOTHING MORE ENTERTAINING THAN A DAY AT THE AMUSEMENT PARK...AND WHAT COULD BE BETTER THAN AN AMUSEMENT PARK THAT IS ALSO EDUCATIONAL?

SO, IN THE SPIRIT OF SUCH CULTURAL EDUTAINMENT MILESTONES AS THE ERECTOR SET, "SCHOOLHOUSE ROCK," AND THE "TREASURES OF ISIS" EXHIBIT AT THE SPRINGSONIAN MUSEUM, I PROUDLY PRESENT *BRAINYLAND!*

RIDES & ATTRACTIONS

BRAIN STREET, U.S.A.

1. Book Mobile Tram Station
2. High Score SAT Arcade
3. Insufferably Avant-garde Playhouse
4. Ten Unforgettable Minutes with Millard Fillmore
5. Whiz Kids on Ice
6. Space/Time Continuum Luge
7. Egghead Mountain

WONK WORLD

8. Einstein's Jolly Genius Jamboree
9. The Geek Islands
10. Pirates of the Internet

The dot over the letter "i" is called a tittle.

SMARTY PANTS SQUARE

11. Ivory Tower
12. Precocious Tots Pavilion
13. Big Bully's Schoolhouse of Horrors
14. Teacher's Pet Zoo

TOMORROW TOWN

15. Corporate Behemoth Runaway Train
16. Carousel of Probability
17. Gridlockotopia
18. The Outsourcer's Apprentice
19. Mr. Mole's Traversable Wormhole

SHOPS & RESTAURANTS

20. The Frontal Lobe Boutique
21. Little Miss Know-it-all Gift Shoppe
22. Smart Aleck's Snack Shack
23. Wunderkind Kaffeehaus
24. Intolerable Child Prodigy Toys and Gifts
25. The Nerds' Table Restaurant
26. The Recommended Dietary Allowance Cafeteria

BRAINYLAND™
The 2,864th Smartest Place in the Known Universe

Let's Ask

Dear Lisa,

I am a ten-year-old boy. There's this girl at school that I like, but I don't know how to romance her. My mom says I'm really cool and any girl would be darn lucky to have me as a boyfriend. Should I have my mom talk to her mom?

Loverboy

I don't think that's a very good idea, Milhouse.

* * * * *

Dear Lisa,

I am so over my current shade of lip gloss. I have been wearing Half-Caf Espresso Cappuccino Lip Gloss as my "signature" lip gloss for six weeks. How do I switch to a new shade without abandoning my core values and compromising my integrity?

Alex Whitney

As Lord Falkland staunchly declared, "Where it is not necessary to change, it is necessary not to change." Staying the course worked for such timeless beauties as Miss Haversham and Zsa Zsa Gabor, and it could work for you, Alex.

* * * * *

Dear Lisa,

I am eight years old and everything in my life is perfect. I don't have a problem with this. I'm just writing to let everyone know.

Janey P.

Lisa! Words to and from the Wise

A "jiffy" is a real unit of time. It's 1/100th of a second.

Uh, thank you for sharing.

* * * * *

Dear Lisa,

I've been in a serious pretend relationship with my imaginary boyfriend for over a year. I recently found out that he has been seeing another girl. I'm not sure, but she might be imaginary, too, which would mean that he has way more in common with her than with me. He says it's over and that he doesn't see her anymore. I believe him, but I still feel betrayed.

Am I crazy to think this way?

Significant Other

Anyone in love is a little crazy sometimes.

* * * * *

Dear Lisa,

My sister is a pointy-headed dweeb who's always giving everyone advice on how to run their lives. How do I tell her what I think without sparing her feelings?

Big Brother

Drop dead, Bart.

Confidential to
Sleepless in Springfield:

You might have better luck if you avoid chat rooms with names like "Bitter, Divorced Fourth-Grade Teachers." :-)

Gossip Department

What eligible bachelor principal was seen sharing an intimate latté in the teacher's lounge with the new substitute third grade teacher?

LISA'S LIFELONG LIST OF THINGS TO DO

- Be unappreciated in my own country, but beloved in France.
- Ride my bike clear across the Great Wall of China.
- Address a joint session of Congress.
- Have my own really cool, hip bachelorette apartment in Capital City.
- Win an Academy Award for Best Screenplay Based on Actual, Breathtaking Events in My Own Incredibly Fascinating Real Life.
- Teach my dad to walk upright.
- Perform the world's first Manx cat tail implant surgery.
- Invent a meatless hamburger that tastes as darn good as a Krusty Burger.
- Find a cure for the uncommon cold.
- Execute a pure glissando from second octave A upwards that causes people to weep at the sheer beauty of its sound.
- Slip the surly bonds of Earth and touch the face of God.
- Learn the ropes.
- Get the hang of things.
- See the big picture.
- Reap what I sow.
- Learn how to program a VCR before they become obsolete.
- Take up some really vile habit so that I might muster the true grit to give it up cold turkey.
- Read every book in the Springfield Public Library.
- Commit T. S. Eliot's "The Waste Land" to memory.
- Figure out what makes Bart Bart.
- Visualize world peace.
- Open the first veterinarian clinic on Mars.
- Have several torrid love affairs and die young, or maybe live to a ripe and feisty old age. (I haven't decided.)
- Climb Mount Everest, but slowly…slowly.
- Master the fine art of casual conversation.
- Learn the intricate dance steps of the Polonaise.
- Save the whales.
- Learn to dance the Hucklebuck.
- Play a sax solo at the Playboy Jazz Festival while protesting the fact that I'm there.

DR. LISA, VETERINARIAN TO THE STARS

TO BE CONTINUED...

MR. BERGSTROM LISA'S SUBSTITUTE TEACHER

Mr. Bergstrom believes that everybody has a talent, something that they can do better than anybody else. Mr. Bergstrom's talent is to be the best teacher one could ever have. He cries while reading "Charlotte's Web," encourages self-expression, and makes fun of himself. With his words, his body language, and his Semitic good looks, Lisa believes everything Mr. Bergstrom says and that there is nobody better than him.

- **Quote:** "A substitute teacher is a fraud. Today he might be wearing gym shorts. Tomorrow he's speaking French, or pretending how to run a band saw, or God knows what."

- **Hair:** Brown and curly.
- **Teeth:** Absolutely perfect—all the way back to the eye teeth!
- **Dress:** Shirt, tie, and jacket with patches on the sleeves.
- **Springfield residence:** The Happy Gypsy (You Pay by the Day).
- **Mode of transport:** Train—traditional, yet environmentally sound.
- **His suggested nicknames:** Mister Nerdstrom, Mister Boogerstrom.
- **New nickname:** The Singing Dork.
- **Educational outfit:** Cowboy hat, kerchief, vest, boots, spurs, guitar, two pearl-handled revolvers, and a belt buckle shaped like the state of Texas.
- **Back-up outfit:** Costume of Copernicus.
- **Special educational snack:** Pemmican.
- **The truth about Jewish cowboys:** They were big guys, who were great shots, and spent money freely.

WHEN I FALL ASLEEP, MR. BERGSTROM IS THE LAST THING I THINK OF, AND HE'S MY FIRST THOUGHT WHEN I WAKE UP.

BLEEDING GUMS MURPHY SPRINGFIELD SAXOPHONE BLUES LEGEND

Bleeding Gums Murphy was a terrific sax player with tons of soul. He came by his nickname the hard way—he never visited a dentist. As talented, temperamental, and unrecognized as only a jazz artist can be, Bleeding Gums was a profound inspiration to Lisa Simpson and a small handful of others and a persistent rumor to everyone else.

- **Quote:** "The blues isn't about feeling better. It's about making other people feel worse and making a few bucks while you're at it."

- **Hit songs:** "I Never Had an Italian Suit Blues," "My Hair Keeps Recedin' Blues," and "Get That Banjo Away from Me Blues."
- **Hit Album:** Sax on the Beach.
- **Local venue:** The Jazz Hole.
- **Favorite place to play:** Sitting on the edge of a bridge during a full moon.
- **Claim to fame:** Has depressed people on all seven continents.
- **Secret shame:** Once had a $1500-a-day Fabergé Egg habit.
- **Remembrance:** His likeness is featured on a panel of the Bouvier Family Quilt.
- **Relatives:** Long-lost younger brother, Dr. Julius Hibbert, and Hibbert's long-lost twin brother, the director of the Shelbyville Orphanage.
- **Turn-offs:** Hootenannies, dentists, and hard candy.
- **Turn-ons:** Jam sessions, Billie Holiday, and mashed potatoes.
- **Memorial:** On his headstone is carved an angel-winged saxophone.

HE TAUGHT ME THAT MUSIC IS A FIRE IN YOUR BELLY THAT COMES OUT OF YOUR MOUTH, SO YOU BETTER STICK AN INSTRUMENT IN FRONT OF IT.

HOLLIS HURLBUT CURATOR OF THE SPRINGFIELD HISTORICAL SOCIETY

Self-described antiquarian, Hollis Hurlbut is not just the curator of the Springfield Historical Society. He is also its custodian and caretaker. Plus, he supplies the voices for the moving dioramas. He is so devoted to Springfield's Founding Father he has developed a serious case of "Jebeditis." Consequently, he'll do almost anything to protect Jebediah Springfield's reputation.

- **Quote:** "Haven't you hurt Jebediah enough, Lisa, with your childish tales of pirate ships and fisticuffs and a silver tongue that can't be found?"

- **Demeanor:** Mild-mannered, professorial, and reclusive.
- **Dress:** Vest, tie, and jacket with elbow patches.
- **Distinguishing features:** Reading glasses and bushy mustache.
- **Favorite snack:** Fresh brewed chicory and microwave johnnycakes.
- **Janitorial skills:** Slapdash and shoddy.
- **Springfield Historical Society motto:** "Where the Dead Come Alive (Metaphorically)."
- **His opinion of the office of town crier:** Nothing but respect.
- **His opinion of Jebediah Springfield:** The equal of William Dawes and Samuel Otis.
- **Notable effects of Jebediah Springfield:** Fife, hatchet, pistol, musket, powderhorn, pipe, mug, jug, candleholder, map, book, money (paper and coin), clothing (coonskin cap, breeches, shirt, and snow boot), and chamberpot.

THE MYTH OF JEBEDIAH HAS BROUGHT OUT THE BEST IN EVERYONE IN THIS TOWN. REGARDLESS OF WHO SAID IT, A NOBLE SPIRIT EMBIGGENS THE SMALLEST MAN.

Sultry, smoky-voiced, millionaire inventor Stacy Lovell is depressed and reclusive. She lives alone in her gated palatial home seeking solace at the bottom of a cocktail glass. However, when Lisa tells her how the sexist marketing of Malibu Stacy is brainwashing millions of girls, she springs to action. Together they create a positive new doll, a doll that will empower little girls everywhere: Lisa Lionheart!

- **Quote:** "I was forced out of my company in 1974. They said my way of thinking wasn't effective. Well, that, and I was funneling profits to the Viet Cong."

- **Residence:** Recluse Ranch Estates.
- **Marital status:** Five ex-husbands: Ken, Johnny, Joe, Dr. Colossus, and Steve Austin.
- **Likes:** Smoking and tinkling the ice in her cocktail glass.
- **Dislikes:** Hideous hair.
- **The Malibu Stacy Legend:** In 1959, homemaker Stacy Lovell had a design and a dream.
- **The design:** Malibu Stacy.
- **The dream:** To mass market a fashion doll that was also edible. Kids didn't much like the taste of dried onion meal, but they loved the doll.
- **Malibu Stacy motto:** America's Favorite eight-and-a-half incher!
- **Bart's alternate names for Lisa's doll:** Blabbermouth: The Jerky Doll for Jerks, Wendy Windbag, Ugly Doris, Hortense: The Mule-Faced Doll, Loudmouth Lisa, and Stupid Lisa Garbage Face.

I'D BE MORTIFIED IF SOMEONE EVER MADE A LOUSY PRODUCT WITH THE SIMPSON NAME ON IT.

MR. DEWEY LARGO MUSIC TEACHER AT SPRINGFIELD ELEMENTARY

As strict about deportment as he is about tempo, Dewey Largo likes his music as clean and well ordered as a Swiss watch. Yet no matter what song his students play, they all end up sounding the same. He deplores minor keys, odd time signatures, and outbursts of unbridled creativity—especially from Lisa Simpson. Despite this, Lisa values his instruction—for its cautionary properties. She even included his likeness on the Bouvier Family Quilt.

- **Quote:** "Do you find something funny about the word 'tromboner'?"

- **Daily dress:** Scoop neck sweaters and clip-on bow ties.
- **Musical avatar:** The inestimable John Philip Sousa.
- **Turn-ons:** Sleeping in a snood.
- **Weapon of choice:** A drill.
- **Secret desire:** To make those football players perform during intermission of his music recital.
- **Claim to fame:** Owns an ivory baton that once belonged to Mantovani.
- **Secret shame:** Wears clip-on bow ties.
- **Didja know:** Mr. Largo has a love/hate relationship with the tune "Pop Goes the Weasel."

HE TAUGHT ME THAT EVEN THE NOBLEST CONCERTO CAN BE DRAINED OF IT'S BEAUTY AND SOUL.

Plagued by Ralph Wiggum's random non sequiturs and Lisa Simpson's continual grade-grubbing, Elizabeth Hoover crams her instructional time with educational films and pointless busywork. She could be described as jaded, but Miss Hoover is more than that. She's also bored, frazzled, weary, disgruntled, and listless. Single and desperate, Miss Hoover is also highly suggestible. She once thought she'd contracted Lyme Disease after hearing about it in all the magazines and news shows.

- **Quote:** "Now, Lisa, everyone needs a blotch on their permanent record."

- **Dress:** Drab.
- **Demeanor:** Dreary.
- **Diction:** Dispirited.
- **Highest praise:** "Yowie!"
- **Hobbies:** Smoking, sighing, staring off into space.
- **Favorite drinks:** Kahlua, Drambuie.
- **Class rules:** No chatter, no gum, no independent thinking.
- **Likes:** Lunchtime, recess, vacations, convertibles, and paintings of boats.
- **Dislikes:** Teaching, monorails, and dissected worms flying up and hitting you in the eye.
- **Social pastimes:** Antique appraising, attending charity bachelor auctions, and playing bridge with the Lovejoys and Dr. Hibbert.
- **Didja know:** Miss Hoover auditioned to be the voice of Poochie.

IT'S NOT MY NATURE TO COMPLAIN, BUT SO FAR TODAY WE'VE HAD THREE MOVIES, TWO FILMSTRIPS, AND AN HOUR AND A HALF OF MAGAZINE TIME.

FROM THE DESK OF LISA SIMPSON:
COMMANDER IN CHIEF

To: The Secretary of Defense
Re: Military Bands

The military band performing at last night's White House ceremony featured an upright bell model tuba. Not only is this instrument overly large, its tone is too deep for "Hail to the Chief." Therefore, by the authority vested in me as President by the Constitution and the laws of the United States of America, I hereby order you to switch to the lighter, sweeter sousaphone with an adjustable front facing bell.

Sincerely,

Lisa Simpson
President of the United States of America, chief executive officer of the federal government, the commander in chief of the armed forces, etc., etc.

FROM THE DESK OF LISA SIMPSON

DESK OF LISA SIMPSON

To: Martin Prince, Chief of Staff
Re: You call THIS a memo?!!

I asked for a short written statement outlining the main talking points for next month's summit. You wrote 300-some pages of single spaced text with no bullet points. Martin, I am trying to run a country here, and I can't do it without bullet points.

Sincerely,

Lisa Simpson,
President of the United States of America

For: POTUS
From: UNKNOWN
Location: SOMEWHERE IN THE W.H.
Message: ASKING FOR AMANDA HUGGENKISS

Returning Call
Please Call Back
Will Call Back X

Take Dad's name off State Dinner invitations list.

National Feed the Squirrels Week
A Proclamation by the President of the United States of America

America's squirrels provide crucial comic diversion for our citizens with their playful antics and their joyful chattering. As we celebrate National Feed the Squirrels Week we renew our commitment to sustain America's most lovable varmints.

My administration has made good squirrel stewardship a priority. Through the Anti-Squirrel Defamation Initiative, we are reducing the number of times these cute little animals are referred to as vermin in the media and by members of my own staff.

NOW, THEREFORE, I, LISA SIMPSON, President of the United States of America, do hereby proclaim this National Feed the Squirrels Week. I call upon all Americans to observe this week with yummy seeds and tasty nut treats.

IN WITNESS WHEREOF, I have here unto set my hand this second day of October.

LISA SIMPSON

To: Bart Simpson, America's First Brother
Re: White House Hotline

Bart, I don't know how you got this number, but please stop calling up and asking for
Heywood U. Cuddleme.

For: POTUS
From: HOMER SIMPSON
Location: SPRINGFIELD
Message: CAN HE BORROW AIR FORCE ONE THIS WEEKEND? PLEASE? PLEASE? PLEASE?
[X] Please Call Back
[X] Will Call Back
Returning Call

• Stay on Message: The truth must Be SOLD!
• Call mom - have her send casserole to U.N.
• Replace cat-scratched sofas in Oval Office

For: POTUS
From: YOUR MOM
Location: SPRINGFIELD
Message: CALLING TO SAY "HI" AND REMIND YOU TO FLOSS

TOP SECRET MEMORANDUM
To: The White House Social Secretary
SUBJECT: The White House Pets

TOP SECRET

Dear Madam Secretary,

America's First Families have enjoyed a long tradition of sharing the White House with a fond pet or two…and, yes, I am well aware of "one or two" being pretty much the limit –historically speaking. Doubtless you are correct in stating that we've never had sixteen cats in residence before. However, while you personally might think that borders on the extreme, I must insist that you stop referring to the President of the United States as "that woman who lives in that house with all those cats."

DR. LISA, VETERINARIAN TO THE STARS

TO BE CONTINUED...

Lisa Simpson's School Project #78
Miss Lisa Regrets...A Self Examination in Charts and Verse

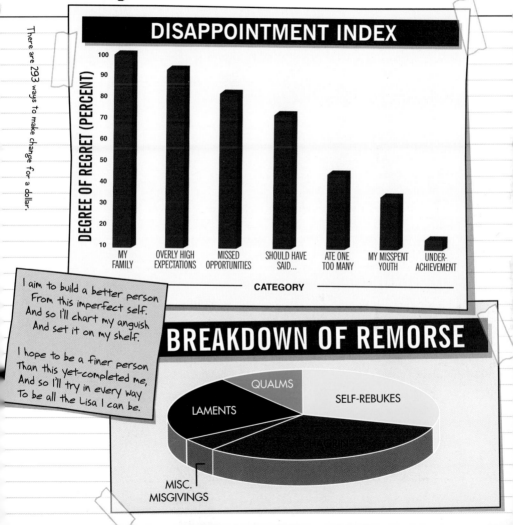

Lisa's Television Viewing Log

- SECULAR SERMONS (Non-Religion) 60 min.   7AM   AGNOSTIVISION

- THAT'S SCIENTIFIC! (Hypereducational) 60 min.
  Kids apply the ideas of quantum mechanics to string theory
  physics then take a nap.   8AM   E=MCTV

- MISTER NOSEY'S NEIGHBORHOOD WATCH (Docudrama) 60 min.
  Mister Nosey blows the whistle on a kitchen remodel
  done without a building permit.   9AM   PUBLIC NUISANCE

- JUST US GALS (Gabfest) 60 min. Actress Jennifer Smythe-Parker
  divulges her secret for beautiful armpits.   10AM   THE CHICK CHANNEL   ▷

- JUDGE MENTAL (Accusatory) 60 min.A woman sues herself for
  eating too much and getting fat.   11AM   GAVELTV

- YESTERDAY'S NEWS TODAY (Rehash) 30 min.   12PM   YE OLDE NEWS NETWORK

- VIDEOTS (Piffle) 30 min. Countdown of the top 10,000
  music videos of the last 25 years.   12:30PM   EMPTY VEE

- SPRINGFIELD ROAD TRIP (Adventure) 30 min. Join host Kent Brockman
  as he sets off on a tour of Springfield's off-ramps.   1PM   PUBLIC EXCESS

- SCREAMING HEADS (Discussion) 60 min. Political punditry
  for the hearing impaired.   1:30PM   C-SPIN

Thelonious Monk is often regarded as a founder of bebop, a form of jazz characterized by fast tempos and improvisation based

IN FRONT OF THE SCENES (Special) 30 min. A look at
the watching of this week's top movies.   2:30PM THE PROMO CHANNEL

THE PATRIOT'S PULPIT (Bombast) 30 min. Self-aggrandizing windbaggery.   3PM FLOX

MONEY-GRUBBERS (Bidness) 30 min. Former child star Corey Bryan
discusses the pitfalls of managing your money.   3:30PM C-SPIN

AFTERSCHOOL DRAMA (Drama) 60 min. Corey Garrett stars
in "The Boy Who Cried 'Hey! Look Out!!!'"   4PM THE CHICK CHANNEL

THE NEWS REPORT (News) 30 min. A report on the top news stories in
the news and a look at why we are saying this is news.   5PM ABCDEFG

SOFTBALL Q&A (Public affairs) 30 min. Mayor Quimby takes the fifth.   5:30PM C-SPIN

WHAT ARE YOU LOOKING AT? (Discussion) 60 min.   6PM FLOX

HE'S SO COREY! (Sitcom) 30 min. Hijinks ensue when Corey's identical
twin cousin arrives from jolly old England! (In a bit of TV technical wizardry,
Corey Stryker plays himself and cousin Basil.)   7PM FLOX

GEEKTREX (Sci-fi) 30 min. Geekdate 0632.7: The Geekship is
intercepted by a ratings-driven life-force bent on spinning
Doctor Sprockett off into his own series.   7:30PM NERDS-AT-NITE

THEATRE OF MASTERPIECES (In English) 2 hrs. The Vicar's Cheese Part XXVI:
After Lady Dredful puts the cheese in the cupboard, Tulk Heffinghorn,
the vicar's scheming solicitor, seeks to uncover it.   8PM   PUBLIC EXCESS

NEWS RODEO (News) 30 min. Yet another round up of today's news and a
sneak peek at tomorrow's top headlines.   10PM NOTHING BUT NEWS NETWORK

on harmonic structure rather than melody.

MY PHOTO ALBUM

by Lisa Simpson, Age 8

I never thought I'd say this, but...
like father, like daughter!

SPRINGFIELD ELEMENTARY REPORT CARD

STUDENT: LISA SIMPSON
GRADE: KINDERGARTEN

Finger Painting — A
Toe Recognition — A
Nap Time — A
Coloring inside the Lines — A
Smock Wrangling — A
Nursery Rhyme Management — A

My first
report card!

(Bart SAYS
this was
an accident.)

THIS
CAFETERIA
UNFAIR TO
DOGS!

My first protest! (I thought corndogs were
made from actual dogs. Mea culpa, Lunchlady Doris!)

HAPPY BIRTHDAY, LISA, OUR LITTLE SUFFRAGETTE!

IN GOD WE TRUST

In retrospect, maybe it was a bad idea to give my 7th birthday party a Susan B. Anthony theme...

BRAN-ADE 25¢

All the profits would have gone to charity (if anyone had bought a glass)!

Slim pickins at my first dance!

LISA SIMPSON

Your most marked characteristic?
My spiky hair.

The quality you most like in a man?
Fire-in-the-belly courage and idealism.

The quality you most like in a woman?
S-E-L-F R-E-S-P-E-C-T.

What do you most value in your friends?
That they don't call me Poindexter Pointy Head.

What is your dream of happiness?
World peace…and a pony.

What is your principle defect?
Mr. Skinner. Hee hee. Actually, that's a bit of wordplay using homonyms, which, as you know, are words that have the same sound but differ in meaning, such as *principle* (a

basic or essential quality) and *principal* (the head of a school).

What to your mind would be the greatest of misfortunes?
Selling out.

What is your favorite occupation?
Self-improvement.

What would you like to be?
President of the United States of America. Or a veterinarian. Or both.

In what country would you like to live?
In a country where there is liberty and justice for all, regardless of one's race, religion, gender, income, or feisty opinions.

Who are your favorite prose writers?
Jane Austen, Willa Cather, and the anonymous, ink-stained, tortured wretch who wrote the *Happy Little Elves Teeny Tiny Library of Itty Bitty Books* series.

Who are your favorite poets?
You just can't beat the Beat poets. Excuse all the wordplay, but at times even I am irrepressible.

What natural gift would you most like to possess?
Ah! The Gift of the Gab — that eternal eloquence bestowed upon those who have kissed the Blarney Stone.

Who are your favorite composers?
Rather than traditional music composition, I prefer the improvised jazz solo that is the hallmark of bebop.

Who are your favorite painters?
The gritty realists of the Ashcan school.

What is your favorite color?
Pink…I think.

Who are your heroes in real life?
Charles Darwin, Bono, and Gwen Stefani.

What is it you most dislike?
I simply cannot tolerate intolerance.

How would you like to die?
Peacefully. Tragically. Memorably.

What is your present state of mind?
Resolute, yet with a subtle air of capriciousness.

To what faults do you feel most indulgent?
Exasperation and self-righteousness.

What is your motto?
The truth must be told. Until then, I'll be in my room.

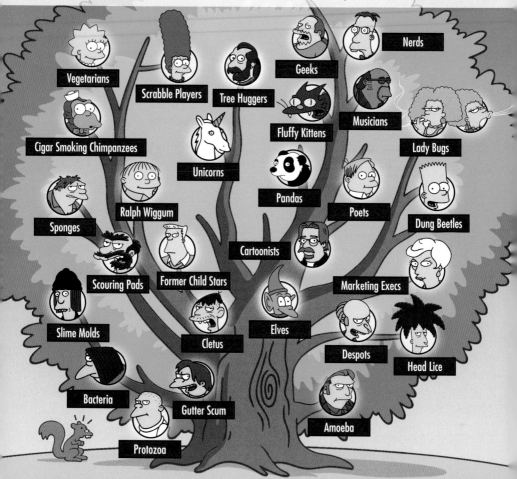

Lisa Simpson, Intelligent Designer

Lisa Simpson's School Project #14

This evolutionary tree depicts life as a progression from lower to higher forms. Although such "trees" have been scientifically discredited, their roots are too well established for them to be easily dismissed.

DR. LISA, VETERINARIAN TO THE STARS

THE END

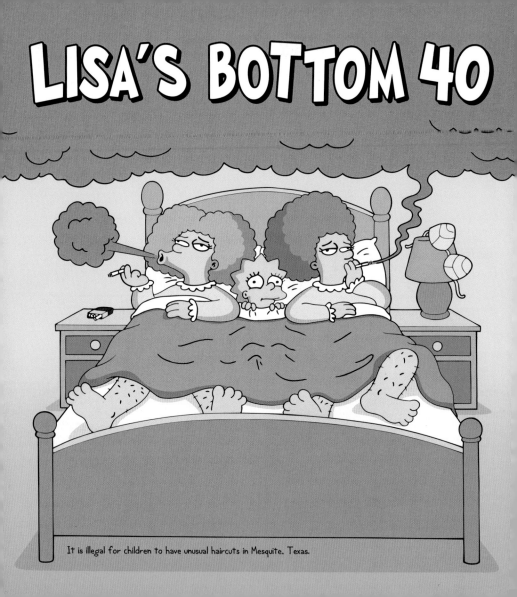

1. Global warming.
2. Tyranny.
3. Mean spiritedness as a path to popularity.
4. Hooliganism as a film genre.
5. Vandalism as an art form.
6. "Wife beater" as a fashion adjective.
7. Overdevelopment masquerading as progress.
8. Truculence as a lifestyle.
9. Ketchup as a vegetable.
10. Mistaking stubbornness for character.
11. Be without the bop.
12. Hip without the hop.
13. Macaroni without the cheese.
14. The unbearable pain of unrequited love.
15. The grim truth that we can't all just get along.
16. First-, second-, and third-hand smoke.
17. Pandering to the lowest common denominator.
18. Evildoers.
19. The Euro.
20. Outsourcing.
21. Sweaters on cats.
22. Cages (unless for batting practice).
23. Cruelty (unless only to be kind).
24. Violence (unless accompanied by really funny sound effects).
25. Treachery and deceit (unless in a romance novel).
26. World leaders who dress in military uniforms.
27. Pimento cheese spread.
28. Losing.
29. When the dog bites.
30. When the bee stings.
31. When I'm feeling sad.
32. Licensing & merchandising gone amok.
33. Despots...and the women who love them.
34. Whacking Day.
35. Schadenfreude.
36. The Taliban.
37. Crushes that leave you crushed.
38. Litterbugs.
39. Carnival barkers.
40. Sleepovers at Aunt Patty and Selma's.

There are four state capitals named for U.S. presidents:

Jackson, Mississippi; Jefferson City, Missouri; Lincoln, Nebraska; and Madison, Wisconsin.